GREAT CAREERS IN SPORTS

by Ted Coleman

FOCUS
READERS.

NAVIGATOR

WWW.FOCUSREADERS.COM

Focus Readers is distributed by North Star Editions:
sales@northstareditions.com | 888-417-0195

Produced for Focus Readers by Red Line Editorial.

Photographs ©: Shutterstock Images, cover, 1, 4–5, 11, 13, 14–15, 17, 19, 20–21, 22, 25, 26–27; Red Line Editorial, 7, 29; Eric Gay/AP Images, 8–9

Library of Congress Cataloging-in-Publication Data
Names: Coleman, Ted (Sportswriter), author.
Title: Great careers in sports / Ted Coleman.
Description: Lake Elmo, MN : Focus Readers, [2022] | Series: Great careers | Includes index. | Audience: Grades 4-6.
Identifiers: LCCN 2021008331 (print) | LCCN 2021008332 (ebook) | ISBN 9781644938485 (hardcover) | ISBN 9781644938942 (paperback) | ISBN 9781644939406 (ebook) | ISBN 9781644939826 (pdf)
Subjects: LCSH: Sports--Vocational guidance--Juvenile literature.
Classification: LCC GV734.3 .C65 2022 (print) | LCC GV734.3 (ebook) | DDC 796.023--dc23
LC record available at https://lccn.loc.gov/2021008331
LC ebook record available at https://lccn.loc.gov/2021008332

Printed in the United States of America
Mankato, MN
082021

ABOUT THE AUTHOR

Ted Coleman is a sportswriter who lives in Louisville, Kentucky, with his trusty Affenpinscher, Chloe.

TABLE OF CONTENTS

CHAPTER 1
Game Day 5

CHAPTER 2
On the Field 9

JOB SPOTLIGHT
Groundskeeper 12

CHAPTER 3
In the Office 15

CHAPTER 4
In the Media 21

CHAPTER 5
Entering the Field 27

Focus on Great Careers in Sports • 30
Glossary • 31
To Learn More • 32
Index • 32

GAME DAY

Many people say the quarterback of a football team is the most important position in sports. That's because the quarterback controls the action. The ball is in his hands on almost every play. When things go well, the quarterback receives most of the praise. When things go poorly, he takes the blame.

The quarterback is the highest-paid player on many pro football teams.

But the quarterback is just one position on a team of players. And it's just one job among thousands in the sports industry. These jobs may not be quite as exciting as playing quarterback. But a career in sports can still be meaningful even if it doesn't involve throwing touchdown passes.

For example, a trainer helps the players stay healthy. An equipment manager makes sure their helmets fit right. A ticket seller makes sure people can attend their games. A broadcaster describes their plays to the fans at home. And when the game is over, fans can read all about it in a story from a sportswriter.

There are many different ways to work in sports. Most of them don't require a strong arm or quick feet. But they do require a love for the game.

A SELECT FEW

Many people dream of becoming an athlete in a major sports league. However, very few of those jobs are available.

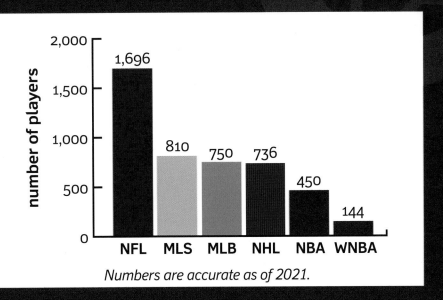

Numbers are accurate as of 2021.

CHAPTER 2

ON THE FIELD

Athletes aren't the only people on the field who help a team win. Every team has at least one coach. The coach comes up with a team's strategy. He or she also works with the players to help them improve. Large teams often have several coaches. Each coach may work with a specific position.

A coach helps players make better decisions during games.

Pro teams also hire people to keep players healthy. For example, athletic trainers help players reduce their risk of injury. To do so, they teach athletes how to exercise safely.

Eating right plays a big role in staying strong and healthy. **Nutritionists** teach athletes about the best foods to eat.

EQUIPMENT MANAGERS

A professional sports team has a lot of equipment. Equipment managers keep all of it organized. They also make players look good on the field. For instance, they wash uniforms and shine shoes. In addition, equipment managers help athletes stay safe. They make sure players have all the protective gear they need.

An athletic trainer may create a workout plan for players on a team.

Mental health is also a huge part of being a successful athlete. For this reason, many players work with **psychologists**. These professionals help athletes deal with anxiety, depression, and other issues.

GROUNDSKEEPER

Groundskeepers maintain a team's playing field. This job means spending a lot of time in the sun. But it is far from easy.

Groundskeepers must have expert knowledge on growing grass. Many go to school to study turf management. They must select the right kind of grass for the sport and the climate. They monitor watering and fertilizing. In cold-weather cities, they must deal with freezing temperatures.

Sometimes weather can change during the game. When that happens, groundskeepers spring into action. They may repair a patch of ground that's too muddy. Sometimes they roll out a huge tarp to keep the field dry. No two days are alike in the life of a groundskeeper.

Groundskeepers make sure the field is in good condition before a game.

CHAPTER 3

IN THE OFFICE

Players and coaches don't end up on teams by chance. A whole staff of people are dedicated to finding the best coaches and players. It all starts with the general manager (GM). This person is in charge of finding and signing talent. The GM puts together the team's **roster**.

Players get most of the fame, but the general manager is the one who puts the team together.

The GM also handles trades and new **contracts** for players.

The GM is just one part of a team's **front office**. There are many other jobs that involve finding and developing players. Many teams are turning to analytics. In this field, people use data to evaluate players. For this reason, teams

SPORTS AGENTS

When handling contracts, the GM usually deals with a player's agent instead of the player. An agent works for the athlete. He or she looks out for the player's best interests. The agent also manages any other business the player is involved in. For instance, some athletes have deals to **endorse** certain products.

Data analysts work with numbers to decide which players will be able to help the team win.

often hire data analysts. These workers look at **statistics**. They try to figure out how good players might be. Data analysts try to spot promising young players before other teams sign them.

Numbers don't always tell the whole story. Teams also want to see players in action. That's why they hire scouts. Scouts go to games to watch athletes play. In many cases, they evaluate players in high school or college. These are the players the team might select in a **draft**. Other times, scouts evaluate other pro players. The scout's team might be interested in trading for those players.

Once a team has all its players, fans want to see them play. That is where a team's ticket sales staff comes in. Some people sell tickets for single games. Others reach out to fans who may be interested in buying season tickets. Ticket sales are a big part of how a team makes money.

Some scouts attend college games to look for promising young players.

Teams also have marketing departments. These workers promote the team. For example, they get people excited to buy tickets. They also work with advertisers. **Sponsors** may want to partner with the team. That way, the sponsors can advertise at games.

CHAPTER 4

IN THE MEDIA

Fans love following the ups and downs of their favorite teams. And there are many ways for fans to get sports news. The people who provide that coverage work in sports media.

Sportswriters attend games and write about them afterward. They usually work for newspapers, magazines, or websites.

Sportswriters may cover college, minor league, or major league games.

 Sports photographers have some of the best seats in the house.

Some writers travel with a team and cover road games. They interview athletes and coaches at games, practices, and news conferences.

Sports photographers take the pictures that go with the stories. They get very close to the action. Sports can move fast.

So, photographers always have to be ready to capture the perfect shot.

Sports broadcasting deals with TV and radio coverage. Most broadcasts have one announcer who describes the action. This person explains what's going on moment by moment. In addition, there is usually at least one analyst. This person gives

TEAM COMMUNICATIONS

Sportswriters don't work for the team they cover. But some teams have their own writers. They might write stories for the team's website. Or they may run a social media account. Teams also have media relations workers to help sportswriters do their jobs. They help arrange interviews. They also provide the information writers use in their stories.

fans extra information. He or she helps the fans understand why players are doing what they're doing.

Viewers at home see and hear the announcers. But the announcers are just a small part of the crew that puts a broadcast together. For example, there are people who operate the cameras. There is also a studio where people direct the camera operators. Broadcasting a National Football League game requires a crew of 150 to 200 people.

Sports news doesn't stop when the game ends. Many TV and radio stations talk about nothing but sports. On-air hosts present the highlights.

TV camera operators wear headphones so a director can tell them what to shoot.

Researchers make sure all the stats are accurate. Writers make sure the scripts are ready for hosts to read. Sports is a huge industry, and there are many people involved in covering it.

CHAPTER 5

ENTERING THE FIELD

Athletes must improve their skills before they reach higher levels of their sport. People with other jobs in sports often work their way up, too. Sometimes they start out with internships. An internship usually pays little to no money. But it helps young people gain valuable experience.

Working for a minor league team is a good way for people to gain experience.

Most people don't jump to the big leagues right away. Some start out with a minor league. Others may work for a college team. Minor league teams often don't have the money to hire a big staff. For this reason, people get experience with many kinds of work.

Education is important for getting a job in sports. The type of education depends on the job. For example, people who work in the media usually have a college degree in journalism or English. Athletic trainers have a background in medicine.

Experience also helps. Former athletes who know a lot about the sport can sometimes get jobs without a college degree. Coaches and scouts are often former players.

Games usually take place on nights and weekends. So, working in sports can mean odd hours. But for people who are passionate about sports, it's completely worth it.

CAREER PREP CHECKLIST

Interested in a career in sports? Try these steps to get ready.

1 Play sports. Even if you don't become a pro athlete, playing sports can give you lots of knowledge about the sport that you can use later.

2 Get interested in the business side of sports. You may already read about your favorite sports teams. But learning the business side of sports can help you figure out what job you might want.

3 Research job opportunities. It may be too early to start working. But seeing what's out there can help you decide what you want to study in school.

4 Become a referee. Youth sports leagues often need people to officiate games. This job can provide a lot of knowledge about the sport.

FOCUS ON
GREAT CAREERS IN SPORTS

Write your answers on a separate piece of paper.

1. Write a sentence that describes the main ideas of Chapter 2.

2. If you couldn't be a professional athlete, which job in sports would you be most interested in? Why?

3. Which person looks at statistics to figure out which players might become successful?

    A. data analyst
    B. groundskeeper
    C. nutritionist

4. Why is it important that sportswriters attend the games they write about?

    A. so fans can ask them questions about the players
    B. in case something happens that isn't shown on TV
    C. so they can cheer for the home team

Answer key on page 32.

GLOSSARY

contracts
Agreements to pay people a certain amount of money.

draft
A system that allows teams to acquire new players coming into a league.

endorse
To publicly support or speak in favor of a product.

front office
The employees who manage the business side of a sports team.

nutritionists
People who are experts on healthy eating.

psychologists
People who are experts on the mind and how it works.

roster
The list of players on a team.

sponsors
Companies that help pay for the cost of an event. In return, the companies get to advertise at the event.

statistics
A branch of mathematics focused on finding patterns in data.

TO LEARN MORE

BOOKS

Hamilton, John. *Sports Photography*. Minneapolis: Abdo Publishing, 2019.

London, Martha. *Legendary Women in Sports Media*. Mendota Heights, MN: Press Room Editions, 2021.

Slingerland, Janet. *Sports Science and Technology in the Real World*. Minneapolis: Abdo Publishing, 2017.

NOTE TO EDUCATORS

Visit **www.focusreaders.com** to find lesson plans, activities, links, and other resources related to this title.

INDEX

agents, 16

broadcasters, 6, 23–24

camera operators, 24
coaches, 9, 15, 22, 29

data analysts, 17

equipment managers, 6, 10

general managers, 15–16
groundskeepers, 12

marketing, 19
media relations, 23

nutritionists, 10

photographers, 22–23
psychologists, 11

researchers, 25

scouts, 18, 29
sportswriters, 6, 21, 23

ticket sellers, 6, 18
trainers, 6, 10, 28

Answer Key: 1. Answers will vary; 2. Answers will vary; 3. A; 4. B